POLISHED ARROW

We are torn, fantastically.

Rayla Noel

Dedication

To the One my soul loves
and us

Preface

"Like a polished arrow,
hid, kept close, concealed
in His quiver.."

" Who - *'He*?" I ask.
These Pages reply.

In the natural world,
we are secure in
Touchables.
We are secure in
visible comforts

~

Acknowledgements

These lines have been inspired by some of the most beautiful people I've met since childhood– a childrens' home by the Bay of Bengal where I first saw abandoned babies and their careful nurture, but also there were those whose faces never outgrew loneliness.

Myra Eski, my artist friend, Mumbai- creek slums; you showed me a side of human courage I never guessed we each have within our everyday lives, where one might look away or just basically help another in need. And Ejnu, a dear acquaintance whose addiction I never forget; my extremely loving family who keep me inspired and cherished: Kitsy for your irreplaceable *Deer & Girl Sketch made* for my "Vineyard of Prayer' Cover Painting, and for being <3 'Naffn' mascot. Vihan my Cheerleader, Angel of song, Consultant on everything and the wow digital work on this Cover! Yona whose blindness turns Challenged moments into polished arrows; Noel my artist- bestie, soul- mate who reminds me of Lord Yeshu -

unravelling mysteries via Change, in everyday events, footpaths & India in all her myriad moments, making me cry, laugh. Thank You God my Father, for life, here and where You are, eternally. And for meeting humans where it matters. Thank you Life, for the shares we've all shared and will continue to. Someone hears human raving in this thing we call Space. These lines are from different people whose faith and guts, are indispensable. To y'all, my Gratitude and unburied grief, my trunks full of unshed laughter, and the healing that follows -

a bruise lets go of comfort;
it can return us, to when
we were little enough –
to sip little green blades
of sun

Title 'Polished Arrow',
Isaiah 49

~

1. Jewel In The Dust

3 am, sky dark, stars stare
heeh am woken by the sound of
a dream smiling; peer thru' the eyelids
of my head, Oi. No one there.

When I was a child I saw headless
shadows (coat hangers),
& talked to *Bambi* - (story book deer
who couldn't stay with her fawn).

Me, I was found in a trash can,
love the open air, I envy footpath sleepers,
they have the universe in their face -
my lips ache for un-shuttered rain;

good girls do not go here and there, Ma Warden says;
maybe there are spidermen in beggars;
psalms in bazaars. Once we watched a Nat-Geo deer,
thirsty for drinking water in the dusty rain. God pl
visit my cathedral of ash! The habit lingers-
they call me *'Smoking Flax',* for my nicotine fingers

~

it is 4 am, in a thick slice of breeze.
'Sweet dreams are made of these,' A poet once sang,
do I need leave my corner
to find You?

Somewhere 'tween this cot and these galaxies
Your scent trails back to me-
without warning- I'm in the room with a Deer
He has sepals and buds in bronze antlers,

fist sized Jewel cluster at our feet-
they dazzle my eyes fighting hard to see
the Deer. All the light in the world breaks in His iris,
like archers.

.

~ *'Seribud Deer'* has antler buds reddening
with dawn, along temples and fawn
gold fur. How do I even know
His name; I'm hearing seeing
seeping images. I, *Smoking Flax*
stare in His amber eyes: they
fill, sparkle. He knows
He knows
me?

some questions are answers
waiting like dawn.

2. It's Hard To Look At You

"Who says you're trash?"
His voice is the silence of suns.
Technically how could anyone like Him
speak to me? (He has antlers)
am grown now, not dream-talking to odd visitors
My fire is a thin ray of shadow, a lamp
with no oil to drink, but the amber twinkle
says He knows, this impossibly tame 'Seribud Deer';
how do I know His name? If you see the sun for
the first time, you'd tremble,
I have that and these sapphire-red-emeralds at my feet.
"Ema," He calls;
can He tell I read in reverse and
spell 'Seribud Deer',as *Bruised Reed?*
"Who calls you trash?"
Don't wish to say who,
His antlers swell in buds, as if with tears
suddenly I'm a sky full of dawn gaudy bird
This won't last: nice things
like sweet dreams leave,
but He is more than a plea,
a request, "S*tay awhile little Ema,*
stay awhile
with Me."

~

No one spoke that way - 'Stay'
except for Maths-mafia, 81 by 9 = 9 .
"Cheh! How you got that wrong,no!
Write that 100times, idiot
homeless, stayherefinishthis!"
Our class monitor's razor-thin 60 degree lopsided grin,
meant to be attractive, was cruel ~
I didn't know the power of my 'homeless'
a vacancy inside filling with emptiness.

—

I visit
my bruise
as Reed's Antlers
begin to throb.
They are a palpable matrix
~of plasma petals;
am touched by their decibels

of colour; a petal for all my
*moments f*rom the beginning-
...to *now*? Raw- buds, every
fantastically bruised for me.
I lean listen, each speaks,
colours, I shut my
eyes to hear

~

*" Say again?
Who calls you
that?!"*

my dorm-sis. I
looked upto her. She
majored in History, I liked
faces of people, doodled them
in pages, back of notebooks....
Dorm sis, starts burning my do
doodles in a trash can; the joke
was/ is a pun, *for fun* everyone
laughed, not just back then but
now....
please
make
me forget, even what I do not
remember. Does an infant absorb
rejection? Or foetus inherit pain?
Warden tells me God is teaching me
something? - Reed is not surprised,
it is just me startled by life.

....

I am thirsty and looking for a
glass of Tall Water -

"Like a deer, thirsts for streams ..."
where have I heard that?)

3. Dove-Bel

Bruised Reed' has the skin
of roses trampled, why does it
even look good on Him, like this
connects us – I watch us -
we are a psalm in a yard,
by a vine press, stream,
yeh my own shadow of valley

"Fear no evil, Dove-Bel," He whispers
(that's 'Beloved'?) He is kind!
What's these Jewels??
like bruises in the sun, they burn shadows,

yelling like a glow,
"Wear them," Reed says -
the ruby – sapphire - emeralds,
scattering light

among gnarling root, leaf.
Heart cries *'Yes!"* Jaw says,
'He wants to own you."
Bruised Reed, shakes head, *"You own me."*

My fingers knot
like in a dream, bare foot
in the Light thru' spined leaf,
this garden full of detached grape:

like they're afraid to hold on,
as if there's miracles, but no takers.
there's a wafer thin moon behind Mr. Seribud
in blue sky, so blue I can swim in it;

~

.....

4. Sparrow

'*..don't trust strangers,*'
Warden Mayami said.

but Mr. Seribud's words wrap like
infant swaddles; never had those.
We were folded in towels, old clothes
and still love floor mats

never had a place
that someone's voice
was in my rib cage ;
am biting curious,
am a sparrow-wide open jaw
asking mouthfuls of answers;
my bars of defence
widen a 360 degree horizon.
He is not man, not angel -
in this woody vineyard, who'd guess
is yards with everybody's secrets–
the old undone, the untamed young, all of us
in the essence of what we may/ may not know :
-tulsi, saffron, spikenard, wild clover,
calamus, cinnamon;

wild flower – they still call me;

                    am tripping back forth back
                    here, a minute is a thousand-

summer vacation, after thin tea
& marie biscuit 2 each, we wrote in our wall
with stem juice from mango-
mayn't sound all bad
but it began my rebellion
I got relief in cutting me
Seribud, Bruised Reed, Sir
I am full of a hollow
He listens with
Archer eyes
I want this chat for a comfort blanket, foreever
but my mind is twisting -vine bark.
"W*ho are you* ?!" I ask,

am not sleeping,
leaning on the sills of my eyelids,
an open window to the sun
Reed has the patience of God, as they
say, "This will take time?" I ask.

"Only Earth has mins, hrs, secs," His sigh is a rainforest
"Neither too short, nor too long are my Hands (of Time)"

Clear Water Stream like a Looking Glass,
ripples my skin. I am
asking, needing to see clear
who is He,
and what I am.

~

Reed, makes me listen to me.
It is unsettling,

~

5. Scar

-i-
I am unruly
like Water: *molecule, three atoms,*
a shape shifter. Me, an ocean between shores,
depths I cannot reach - He walks waves
to me. His words are dancers in my storm
– He is Questions that answer;

"D'you know the womb of the sea?
Has mist a father; from whom does the frost
of heaven, offer thunder for desert rain..?"
"What's that to do with my pain?" I ask
He is still; crown
to floor - the floor oh the floor is a
whrrring movie screen,

a million billion grains
of shore at a sea of salt
 tears - ours. Tears, torn places,
I'm listening in His ears,
they beat our pulse, in dual

decibel from the inside

When He speaks, it *is* the silence of suns -
"Who knows the way of Light? It
cannot be pinned, travels186,000m/ sec
it dwells in a Way, a Path
mingling with none."
I nod nod, inside my jaw
He's where aorta & breath-blood sieve,
"Can you, human,bury
wickedness in the dust?"
"uh."
(not saying more, I can only perceive).

-ii-

"You have pierced snout
of crocodile or bullock snoring
under lotus tree? Even they
were made by Me... soft loud, gentle
harsh, wild tame, sweet bitter

I fumble, *"Everything is Yours, na.."*
The Reed's smile is naked noon – daze -
His words are a two edged sword, in my

layers of memos: they congregate in
my teeth, like prayers waiting to speak.

He speaks as God ?!–
 Who else asks
"Bless those who hurt you,
and I will accept your prayer,"

...do *what* for them
them - dumping me in trash
for being a girl, or being born
at all?

"Forgive them because
the act frees you
from toxic, cyclic
unforgiveness. "
He says

Sure – I'm thinking He
doesn't have Freudian memory
of belly of garbage bin in face;
"...what d'you know of mercilessness?"

-iii-

"What do I know of mercilessness...?"

He is stories I've read. Now
am watching the Past in the Present,
how does He even know me, even if this is a
dream, it is important-

(At the court hearing, there was release of a
criminal – named Barabbas, for the life
of this Yeshu, (Jesus). I'm seeing that,
'm seeing me, as that other criminal
* A transaction - He was Bruised,*
died for Humanity, Ah, thats, The
"Bruised Reed"; thought that was
only a Holy phrase. Then again
He took my place, I see,

I'm-a- shut-up-prayer- in- a- prayer ,
not cast out, no bars. His eyes are the morning
star; I am the dust of runaways

He takes us back
to a rock -
scarring with names:
– like news headlines
running neon in the street,

names, names, scores, a thousand
million huddle. and mine and His, "*Yesu*" – (*SeribudDeer*)

He morphs into a kneeling man,
Yes, I have recall, I've heard this before:
with other heroes, martyrs, kings,
poets, sages and monks, of cities buried and
ghosts of wars, dust narrating destiny. But this
One speaks His lips - with my name in it,

~

what sweet thing is this Hope?
Abstract, like a painting I don't understand;
how can God be both God and illustrative Man?
Please, let's re-visit This

~

6. Chest Full Of Tesra

outside my door
there's a mosaic of chappals
(hostel mates and mine).
Warden Ma says people can be odd
"N*eed for their approval will hurt you.*"
I search for peace in the beach
hunt Joy in guava tree.
love, in the monkey's little darty eyes,
in mango blossom, they allow you to be fragile

we pass yard gate to the shore,
Uh, is it really the salt of all our tears-
Seribud nods head, *"Yeh, what d'you say?"*
A seagull glossy in the sunburnt sands, replies,
"Naffn naffn,"
if this is a dream, that's fine!
I can be me. No apology.

The Deer's white hide has a chest of "Tesra",
oh t-e-a-r-s?

Reed nods at that, and at my memos:

they congregate in my teeth,
like prayers waiting to speak.
"H*ow's the cough?"* He asks;
a crystal wind runs through me
When I wore sport skirts, my scars showed;
I'd say they were from an accident

at High school not everyone was without an actual home

~

I'm face down, floating
not just tired, but alone
I see steps, Someone. Walking the water to me-
Who walks water?
Where's the Deer gone, I understood Him a little.
The feet I see now are a Man with holes in ankles
please. He bends Face bones to me; like waves,
surround, lift, lull, I am what I was, but look at me
now.....
I am like water between shores
He walks that water to me.

We return to that Rock
scarring with names:

~

this is like a hiding place...

21

7. @ Kneeling Rock

-i-

a mosaic of names, running like
neon news lines, filling
by the second

names in this
Kneeling Rock run
: *Mira, Nani, Bopu, Datu,*
billion billion names in exchange for His,
are scratched with nails of a breaking Hand
Bruised Reed, He morphs into a Kneeling Man

~

they fed us mashed pumpkin,

boiled rice. Later at *Shanti House*
for Children of Joy, Warden Ma said
I should've been a boy – there was a
couple that'd 've taken me, hoooh!
I grew to be ***'Smoking flax',-*** some of us have
nicotine stains. Maybe my Bio Ma smoked;
my questions hang from the ceiling fan, they
spin whirr, rootless plants swimming in deserts
I do not hate anyone; how do you dislike an unknown
face

just wish I could erase other's mistakes
that scar my arms and feet, my fear of anything
sweet, and also erase my indifference -
if wishes were prayers, and lips, petals
I'd be a sunflower, turning to the sun

-ii-

THIRST

the light is crushed grape

                                        colour of vine
                                         in a sip,

I'm wearing a thin cotton wrap burning
                            900 degrees C
                           with my smoke

                        my nicotine nails,
                               they nail
                                 me in

        In a Cup to drink, He pours my
        *coffin-nails** they tear His throat
        with a cry that startles, the star
        long ago over Bethlehem -

                  time lapses forward back
        He has much to fill in the gaps
        Why would God drink my mess?

*"Have you humans sacrificed something
        you want for something you need*

not just in your temples - winged creatures, sheep,
or ram's blood, your time, sleep, joy
there's always a living sacrifice

"I'm that, for you. You, humanity
the Cup demonstrates
I've consumed your hell
Gave up my Will, for this.."

He's getting in my scars,
-this place we shut out
things we cannot see

(He gets our slang for a cigarette?*

(have you cried out 3 am - ish
not dreaming there'd be Reply?)

a cry,
is a
ray
falling
up
ward

~

8. Not Carnal Instinct

not the breathless at a marathon,
not the tired of exams sweating you,
not of taxes unpaid, or auto driver's face
or saggy waiters end of day, the huddle
of lawyers at iron wrought gate
I am tired of doubts
they insist, *'.. hurt wont go.'*
They say these are my much earned scars,
why heal - & that *'True Love'*,
happens only to movie stars,

God, I need settle bad done
take me to the secret place of Your
heart, where the only outcast
is fear;
by that stream at rock yard
we look in, the grass is dew
but the face in my head is
broken. *"Nah that's not you,"* Reed
says. *"That is borrowed Fear."*
Fear wears my face?
My unsettled 5'4" inches
Fear saying, I let it rent my head
my soul,

"You believe Lies?"the Kneeling Man,
shoves my terror Tenant (Fear) in a
yawning black hole. What is that?
"Hell," He replies, and then writes
me in the palm of His Hand,
"Ema" (not Smoking Flax),
next to His -'Yeshu'.
"Though you be as dark
little scar-lets, watch it in
a Fountain Fall, for you....."
Fear looks on, mimes a hug!
"I'll hang around, if you still have
room to Let?"

the deepest ravines are
inside.

HOODIE

vertical lines in my marooned lips
are not rouge velvet of lipstick,
but the smoke my bio Ma gave me;
I do not have questions about her face
you cannot miss what is not yours,

though pieces of me now and then, object
I don't know if I'm old or young.
My birth certificate is in yellowy paper,
the colour of our cook's turmeric cheeks
she's a kind of mother, heaping spoons of
tomato rice beans in plates that must erase
the sins of everyone
I am 3 years old. Or 17 or 24 or 31

or a millennium of a thousand trees of ancestry
it is extraordinary to never know if my paternity
is in fact butchers. Imagine the billion wings
and feet they've done: nothing against any person;
if we were to add up all our mess, it would battle the
stars,
it is hard to take my hoodie off;

warden Ma says I am good to be a teacher
but, ugh, my anxiety! - even after years in Psychology
Class.
Maybe I should work with those Special children
4 mins from my hostel with 20 beds for 20 girls, here
our 20 steel plates washed in bore-well water;
with the children there, watercolour running down
paper
meeeeh, their bow lips asking, asking,
their chocolate fingers tag you to the wash, the dining

they stick in your mind, why do people have rights
to ask about your life -

they smell it in my collars and sleeves full of Marlboro
I am still on charity Rehab packs. When it is pitch dark,
a person can go guilty at being born. Invisibility
is easy, in your Hoodie and any hiding place
Why'd You start this..like a Deer?" I'm unable to open
eyes,

He is ultraviolet transparent! *"You love Bambi.*
You understood better when I looked like that.
Memory helps fill gaps....." The Light in Him is 360
degrees
here there is no shifting shadow...

faith is an instinct
birds and babies,
the very old, the dying ,
the dead see

~

9. No Shifting Shadow

at

school there was
a bell, there was a song,
a hallway, sacred verses,
'As the deer pants for water
my soul longs after You ===
The Chapel had a gold dusty
foot pedalled organ, in the corner .
Stained glass Shepherds and sheep
looked down while we sat in rows or kneeled,
I thought praying looked like sipping clear water

****

****

****

......

I'm thirsty
not for mountain dew soda

I am meters of parched pavements, walked for answers,
but the questions sit in rows, they stand in the gaps
like people in rush hour bus, in my city,
faceless commuters, or in the foot board, ready to get off
only I cannot get off
Unsure why
I cut myself, it was my safe house with closed door
the Deer, is the Man at the Kneeling Rock, and is God
He uses what you know, and He knows my
questions
I am burning alive from the tips of fingers,
to the smoke in my tongue
Warden prays the 'sickness' leaves me.
I am sick?
I am.
I stare at Him through
doors unable to open
He makes me,
somehow transparent -

"I've watched you from childhood Bambi Tales
wove you in the secret place."
"You sound a thousand thousand years old!"
"I am!" He grins in eastern tanned skin
How can God be nice Deer illustration,
and Man; chaotic even for a dream,
 oh what can I ask if I knew
I'd be heard,

what ask God?
There be conditions to apply?
"Yes," He says.

~

faith is a bell
you can hear
in the dark

~

10. Sip

Unsure I like this

*..He says ..***"Bless those who sin against you, and I will accept your prayer.**.." Say
what for them dumping me in trash 'cause
I'm a girl or they just didn't want me
for what-ever, they go free,
being irrespon
-sible, &
all?!
I'd
wish
them
harm
back!
*"No. No. No.
Forgive them!!"* But why would I *???!!!*

I cannot stop my rage
this is not against Him or any!
The injustice of it, is venom
and I don't want to drink any cup a snake spat in!
"Forgive them," the Bruised Reed whispers,
it takes humility to forget self, to push thru
the worst, and never stop; its to be a star
over the storm, thru' revolutions of change,
eclipses, all this forgiveness business,
then 'blessing them' ??

~

It

frees

you from

the venom of unforgiveness. "

"Sure." I reply. "You don't know what it takes, to have

Freudian

memory of belly of garbage-bin in my face;

" *...do I have Freudian memory of...?"*

He laughs tears, bitter sweet, like a

baby in very coarse bed clothes

I get the feeling I've asked too much,

but His face is a crinkling map of Joy -

of tiny birthing shelter, straw, bleaty sheep

startled shepherds, big star that drove three

wisemen and a king (murderous) to do things

history wouldn't believe: a bitter cup, Son of God,

a Cross,

a....

King - sized sacrifice.
He leads my stains
out past the vine -press gate,
there's no sweet water here
just the death hiss of a whip
a Cat-o-9-tails, slish cut slish.

Watching You organise Your Will,
Kneeling Man, I see it shred You
slap cheek. pant breath, whiplashes 40;
Deer 'Hind of the Morning', as they call
You - Friend of Sinners, Yeshu. I
guess even I'd run from this scene
this scene that tears Time, in BC/AD
& You ask me to surrender my Will

it will rip me in shreds I can't hang out
to dry; wish I were inanimate, a clothesline....
anything but me, dear Jesus. No offence, but inside

these 206 bones, I wish I were a field of sunflowers,
involuntarily turning to You. That'd be so easy

I'm human
a woman,
can You birth me
again?

"A mother ......may forget
her child but.... I've carved
you in the... palms of
My ....
Hand
<3

~

& "Bless" is a word I
do not like

~

11. Tattooed By Grace

held by what never let go
I hold on

at 'Skull

hill '..

Its not

nice;

there's nails in His hands and Feet holding

Him at a Cross, and a spear in His side

but He echoes,

Father

forgive

them

they

don't

know

what

they

do :

'm getting a
life sized hint, to go
and forgive someone.
sure, I am just t' pickle
of dying meteors and trua-
-ma - Yes, You hold me
in Your Cuts & want
graft me in!
Blest tragedy -
God's
Son died
for me?

"pinned like a rose, on the Cross,
He was thinking of me. "

~

" your sins, though red as scarlet
can be white as fresh snow..."
<u>*My sins - I'm*</u>
sinner?!
And all those people in my life -
they ...?

~

we trace cellar stairs to the basement
of me. It is hard to see the winding rusted stairwell
hard to tell how steep, narrow, spiralling this is,
my years, going down to zilch, no traces, no race
no origin, no sweet altar of grace?
Yes, just pink cloud candy saturdays at
the gate. Some of us thrived on the love we gave,
the rest of us loved
with the love we did not receive

and learned to know Love cannot stay,
emptiness, was familiar, safe.
Untrustworthy, would not leave,
it couldn't.
This emptiness of unfilled things:
albums - no baby boots-
my rooms with no older people
that are mine –
my spiralling downside
never mind the rust,
whats the emotion of a person missing something,
they search lane, shops, counters, faces
words said/ not said;

a person can conclude they're conceived like a sin,

the villain. I, the evil I'm running from. In a storm,
I'm a lighthouse but my rays are the night!
'How dyou talk this way/" Warden asks in tones
that mistrust everything except failure.

I've had little sacredness;
there's a bowl of petals in the 'Peace Room'
and some amount of sweet chapel sundays-
have you been the invisible one in the room,
they're talking but no one's talking to you,
have you been a voice no one hears:
thats how I've always seen prayers
: mumbles in the chin. So I have preferred
to not, mumble

now I see Light pursue the dark as if
to save it from its own darkness if It could,
the sun spinning round us all 365 x n
seeking the night, but the dark - even in me
runs hides, hides, photophobic, maybe,
though now am being tattooed
: like a shadow to a foot

~

12. Vertical Acres

"You should be dead,"
I'm thinking.
The Man
on the Cross
His body white ash,
in noon rain lashing, lashing us all:
through an invisibility I can see; our
earth shifts shape under the sky......
it is a dragon of noise, it slams .... in
my ribs. The Man is somehow me?!
I look up at the Cross beams, the
nails tear out of Him, the light is
the colour of crushed balm
for on wounds
that heal.

scars are rungs.
They-take me higher.

it can be many things,
but a scar is vertical acres

when I forgive,
I'm still torn

but
fantastically

~

*"A bruised
reed He will not break
and a dim burning flax,
not snuff out!"*

I stare at His Words

the Word stares back

Compassion's colour is a Jar of clay
full of His life.
The Colour of Forgiveness is
a broken Body pouring out
Redemption: a Live transaction

more than the giving of alms, and
coined vow -food fast
& penances
The Colour of Healing,
is a bruise pouring out,
why does He care
so much??

+

·

.

shine
~ more than
iced dew, or falling
stars, There are Jewels under
.....the rust of us. When a man, child.....
woman prays; when we weep
when we kneel, we're more
than what we believe
If we could see
ourselves in
the Light,
of His
Ey-
-es

.

.

but doubts happen, gnaw gnaw
rats and fox, in the yards, with saw for teeth.

13. Beauty & Beast

who am I
who is this

"Shut up and be!"
She has blue eyelids, the pupils are pools
deep swirl tides, her skin raw gold in refiner's coal
~ the shade of stripped branch in monsoon dawn,
her voice, the husk of grain slapped down-
it scrapes my throat. I know her name is *Apni*
the fingers long, they wrap my lungs
my scream sears navel, sole, the hours
are minutes are seconds. She sifts stains off my nails.
I'm torn like fruit premature from branch, her smile the
chill wind, december mist - *Apni* unleashed,
shaves the bark off my teeth,
pulls me, out of me, She is beautiful but a beast

I try call the Deer's real name
the kneeling Man at the Rock
One at Skull Hill that walks again
in the Garden for those that find Him, this I know -
even if I cannot believe it all, and yet
before I call, He is here,

"You know Apni?" He goes:
"I too read reverse like you.
'Apni.'
Decode her."
A-P-N-I... heeeh! P-a-i-n.

"Not an entire enemy, Apni has been
with you, long. Don't let her scare you."
I want to scream, "Enough! I just
need to breathe..."

can't undo what makes me smoke
why do I need it? Why was I conceived in what I am
cant you Lord of Everything
un- do, unbirth, or
birth me again.... ?

Apni holds me in endless arms - me,
dim wick that I am;
her fingers break strip naked
every extra leaf
in me;

my voice and I fall in echoes
scattering in tiny pieces of darkness.
Apni leans back inside my lungs.
She's leaving as I exhale,

inhale, exhale, inhale, sip on sip
of clear water grass dew
till I'm a green field full;
Apni waves,
she is happy, work done,
I want to say thank you
but who thanks Pain

between pillar and door, like a jealous love,
am held onto, by the Truth of Truth
" Set Me as a seal on your heart, for
there are the wolves Beloved,
child, mine, set me as seal on even your
pain..."

this is not what I expected to do,
but am to my last dregs of thirst,
can't help grab What's grabbing me - unthinkable Cost,
The rugged Cross, pouring quenching
in my thirst. How'd He even visit me?

WHO AM I
149.6 million km from the Sun, radius 6,378 k
I, Earthern Jar in space held by Grace

~

14. Hurts That Heal

tell me something I do not know
about me,

Sir God
He says nothing, it is so loud,
let my face in the iris of His Palm
I turn
a page at the narrative
in His foot bones
the stake in His side
crown of thorn in Temples
they re-write my name,
"Beloved, Be- Loved....."

the Word leads me by streams of streets,
places I never knew I've been -
"I was there where you were born,
knew your name before the foundations of earth
gardens and civilisations and hell...",

~

~ first baby pic, 2 months old, hospital
snapshot, rescued by a kind old lady
too old to care for me, she gives me to the House,
in woollen shawl she knit. It was winter
Indian humid salty rains, by the sea,

in the ICU, near a yellow walled
'House of Joy,' they grew brinjal,
sweet potato. Ghee rice every, 6 months: I still hear
kitchen sieves, paddy husked for home breads;

we are moments, unsaid
*branch on branch,
leaf bud, blossom, curl of baby
tendril hair, vine
clasp, graft, wrist, palm

~

all this is too much to chew on
but *branches do not chew -
I understand, grafting hurts
new raw flesh over a wound.
Have you watched a Graft or heard this line

I can't get off my head : a hurt that heals a hurt that
heals.
Rehab hurts
new babies hurt
new mommies hurt
the friendless hurt
the friendly hurt
we are full of much need,
we do not shut our doors to evil
we harvest rain, sow clouds
we capture sun rays for our baths,
snap fingers for lampshades
we all graft into some sap or the other-
'self-made' is a myth, ask a test tube baby.
I understand that Hope is sweet and distant
like sky blue seeping in window edges,
I'm a prisoner, a prisoner of hope, unsure how
but just willing to shift my dust to destiny,
& Be- loved

~

saw dew drop hung on rust rail,
saw girl with pearl earrings
(they're made from oysters?)

that pearl is still a drop of
ocean dust?!

53

....Scars are
shape- shifters......

15. 3 Jewels & Their Thieves

Love sinks outward

as a Jewel does, seeping in
edges with Light, reflecting the sun,
spark of my inner weave, re- wiring.
It is precious as **Faith,** I must wear as
Shields! The colour of emerald-sapphire-
ruby. You triplet of **Hope** & Love. Have I
not known, you are the heirloom I been
looking for, entirely! Have I treated y'all
disgracefully? Have the villains in me,
thieved you over and over, I'm so so v.
sorry, my precious, stunning ones, I
will try clasp you to the nape of my
pain – no other burden carry me
Will try hold you in the wrist
of my scars, a
a pendant to
trauma; oh
you three
Beauties
never let
me go, or
forget I am
your keeper,

~

When Reed laughs

it is the " *Ayoooy*!" of delivery,
mid-wife clapping blood palms,
If I could choose a birth,
I'd get the DNA of this moment!
But who chooses Destiny- we
puppet, mannequin dressed
by commerce, cannot undo
who I've been but can, what
I will be ?

hems we undid, re-stitched. Towels labelled,
" *Girls House.*" Shoes in families of sizes-
us in a family of bleach-washed pillow cases.

"Be grateful, be humble." Principal S.N. Matu said.
"Of course, amen." We replied. I shrugged inside
from so-called sacred; we were untouchable;
Hotel man sent breakfast one Saturday a month
graciously reminding us how good life was to us -
we could've been -*God knew where*, he said.
I mistrusted God, whom they talked of as the
source of my safe house

Sundays were straight back benches in rows
hot candle wax in our fingers, we needed
to pay for the sins of our fathers, mothers,
whoever. We were one House name
'Children of Joy'. I embroidered
the words* in collar and kerchiefs for sale
at yearly NGO fests, every October
there were crackers , fountains, chakras of light,
sweet chariot boxes of 'death by chocolate', not for us.
One lady went, " ....*poor child!"* She lined her lips
purple in a tiny oval mirror, smiling at her
talcum cheeked perfection

I feared human varieties of gods and

goddesses, & those worshipped
in mirror and glossy magazine super
heroes/ heroines, pouting a love
that wore neon blouses, gucci
and celluloid songs for tickets
sold in queues, and malls with bald head
mannequin: armless, frozen staring
in space. I learned that I seemed untouchable
by any kind of grace

~

*peace
is a kiss
from
heaven*

~

16. Eternal Perspective

before I speak, I'm heard
before a tear falls, it is
shed

they take Him
to a yard of
the grave, but
see my name !

"Smoking Flax
no longer lives,
Crucified
with Christ,
free of stain.
IF SHE
WILLS!!"

"Wh...uh????
I SO WANT NO
NON- SENSE
IN MY LIFE, but

be birth, again?
.........heeh

:
my
wick,
smoked
out blue-black
like His Body. His
stains are a blood
belt on mattress of
spices; flax fibre
covering
me

*"Why bother counting our punches, yours
or mine; they're all taken,"* He smiles;
ne'er heard a Dead man rising! &
Wounds that could heal! His :

flax linen, wrap reminds -
e'en I, birth again?

in a clutch, of baby fist,
my void pushes in labour-
contracting contracting my
final shove into a world
I've never been part of,

He hears my invisibility:
the noise of human assessment;
a bruise is where we shut up what we
cannot see, but no more.
never had a place
that Someone
stayed in my rib cage
(I've worried that
if in the end,
there is nothing, then
why care,, why work

why need love, why heal
why the desperation for
repair, for inclusion
for salvation, why is the
human heart so easy to break
when its all so tough anyway;
what is the purpose of
peace, when there's war,
why have life, when there's
going to be only death -
& what do the dying see);

I've seen one,
in our campus clinic
he went as joyfully as the
life he lived
hostel gardener, lost left leg in
a storm, he used to be a fisherman,
then he grew rose trees
and picked almond leaf
for the school aquarium.
Uncle Gopi we called him,
where did he go
what made him happy before he left
sang songs with his sand paper throat,
we asked him to stop, but his laughter
made us laugh, I miss him....

The Bruise
is silent,
makes me listen to me,
"...
the whole thing about this and you and Gopi
is everyone gets to live forever, if you don't let
let you - go to hell. You have a choice
this doesn't stop here, Ema,

~

         He holds me up
         form the inside

~

      I am not a poet, I'm a poem;
       & all negatives wait for
          the Light

~

17. Temptation

wait -

this is my hell?

For a nano second, there's an eclipse -

the light is black fire

in front of me is a Person completely - darkness,

head to toe little scales of bone ash sawing at itselves

wailing, deathless, *"Call me 'Slie'! You'd know! Uncode*

that, read that reverse or don't!"

SLIE - LIES? (who ?) We're burning alive, forever.

"Wheeee heeee!" tongues of flames exit Slie's face.

"I'm pure evil, wow, the insane, oxymoron!"

"You love your coffin-nail tobacco, don't you?

You born that way....nobody's Babe!" With each flick of

his cheek,

Slie sends tiny whirlpools

of fire - they rave, gasp in me,

the craving starts

a small jaw in the back of my head.

Slie 's eyes are hollows filling with the ash dropping

off my hand. *"So........say 'Yes', no?!"* crawls close.

I see tiny skull shaped embers, in a living, writhing
necklace.
"These are my EJWELS, yah???! (He can't mean Jewels),
"Mah precious souls," Slie hoots, the echo hollows
in a throat made of jaws, more than I can count. He is
hunger, and thirst

I'm racking gagging in the sulphur salad we're in,
then I see Him - like a Deer, nimble on my coals,
leaping to me -
the sky and its grades of blue, smash right thru
the Deer Man in His own Shroud, now trans-physical
His blood, red as lambs', pours through the iron zips
of the mouth of Hell closing in
"Lies!" The Bruised Reed cries,
"Remember, this Lamb's blood
is only antidote to your snake poison?"
He erases Slie bending circles at my feet-
"This Baby Girl was never yours. Liar, liar, liar, she's
Mine."
I'm walking through photons,
resurrection radiates me,
umbilical Chords bond;
the music of Healing - nothing missing, nothing broken,
what just happened? The Great Delivery!, but

Lies make me believe
a Heart eclipse lasts
forever,
zero repair

~

the War of all War is over our Soul

18. Bruised Reed

let me be the dew drop
that warns => the Light
will soon be
too much
to look at

a tomb full of Life
a stone, rolled by lightning -
a grave situation,
-broken

want to touch Him but I fall like wax, I
scatter.
Want to touch Him,
His Eyes of fire, lit
florescent 4.3 X 1.1-m, linen flax burial cloth chars
to a thin sheet of carbon, He arrives off all sides, and
assembles,
@ resurrection.
It is not what a human can see, or believe
just Breathe if, need t
I want, want it

for me too, I need it -
my old, me-
like a seed, buried dies, raises its head, through
the floors of Self, thru potholes and places
i wouldn't know to tell.

"A New Day!" He
re-traces stairs to my base via a glass darkly, I read, see
as if the first time,
my face- jaw bone on neck, heart, lung
aureoles of existence –
here there is little anger left, only radiance.

"I have a Gift for you," The Reed is more
than I can respond to now -
He's got me fresh linen, Flax!- stitched with threads of
light
and words, *'Mili – Tyhu'*

"Heeh!
Like you'd say, but
so you'd remember
child - wear this one with Joy,

like daughter of the King
carry it like a Shield, wear it like a Crown-
breathe deep in the Aroma of Grace
wear it as Faith's armour to your soul,

for your own voice may instruct you
to be afraid.
Humility will tell you
" Perfect Love casts out all Fear'

Perfect Love trembles only in the presence
of True Love
and that Love is all that remains,
here

The Reed glows with Light that puts out the dark,
He pours the Morning Star in the little lamp in my heart,
and all
the sky outside, turns into one mega Face of
-Father

" *Set my face to You,*" the Dove-Bel I am (in my new
spirit) whispers;
the more she (I) looks at Him, the more everything dims
till He shines in the ashes of what-
of what was.

~

WHAT THE OUTCASTE PRAYS

the outcaste pray from an untouchable place,
none know- except the untouched, for they are the child
of the unknown;
when the untouchable pray, who hears, except
the God of all flesh, Who goes where angels couldn't?

Yea cast out everything that's hung chandeliers of curse
I've been an outcaste too long in my own house.
Did I subscribe to the wind, then go now four winds
thru' the Fire-mills of God; Oh Lord,
stamp me with Your recognition

~

setting up a **'Trespassers will be prosecuted '** *sign :*
"Trespassers of tree cutters,
weed planters, thieves, foxes, rats
leave,
or forever,
shushhh!!!"

~

I did not find You in altars of milk
but in the little gully behind heart break

19. Twins : Grace & Faith

**Faith looks up
Grace replies**

Her skin raw -
burnt by a million
millions days, nights;
her hair -the roots of ripe yellow mustard bud.
*"I live in cells and bars, prisons,
and with you now.
You'd read me as THAIF,
I am Faith!"*

'm staring my face off.
She is stunning lovely, fragile
but you don't want to mess
with that look in her eyes,
she can look thru anything,
" *Thaif,* I mean, Faith, really?
I have *you?*"

When Faith smiles,
her skin peels like a tree in Indian summer.
"Remember These?" the Light in her falls
shimmers on the Three Gems, like
like night stars in her fingers –

but what is that scary thing
in her strong hands
a diamond studded carving knife
you'd think someone called Faith
be tender!

" What's with you?"
I'm screaming,
Faith begins carving out
every last of my
shifting shadows:

they curl out of me, our wisp, with every twist
hard as diamonds the more she scalps them

out of my skin, the lighter I feel,
but indignant

:

1.Self- hate
2. Mistrust of love,
3.My charges
against All.

"These are mine, they're
old friends,
they're what I've gathered
all this time, this is me, this is mine!" I scream

"OH?"
Her long brows arch
right at
where
I rebel.

"I'm going back to the Cross,
to pin these, there.
NEVER take them
down again
please."

Not to argue with Faith
I say yes,
then remember,
this is that Place of
-no shifting shadow

~

Movement under the dry leaves
a Crawlie, Creep crawl creeeeeeep crawl
leaves. "*What's that?*" I ask,

"Slie!.."
Grace, replies. She looks like

Faith, but her skin is gold fire that
can burn hell with her own warmth
if she would:

Faith's twin,
*"I am Grace – you'd maybe
remember me best as
'Ce Rag', neh?*

I'm slow to un-jumble that,

its been a lot here, and I can't help
seeing all my 'Goodness' as filthy rags
next to these Beauties, and ..
I remember the new Linen gifted me:
Humility, Humility, softens me,

Grace waits waits, waiiiiiits
waits, reminding me speechless,

Grace is- *the 'Undeserved favour of God',*
.......dares-devils, her touch is the aroma
of new rain on drought : the very Breath
of God, e'en the greatest Emotion:
forgiveness

"Hmm,
what crawled away is Slie - Mr.Lies,
past tense for you, but that Deceiver will keep trying-
as long as you wear your Three Gems, no sweat!"
She feels tough, but she's the sweetest
to breathe with

the Gems glow in the dust
scattered around as if no one cared for them.
little darling destitute legacies, like
clustered there, waiting for me

" ..and Reed,

the Deer Man, He
said there are others, as these
precious to His soul
...?"

"Yes, He would say that,"

with fingers fast, too quick for me
Grace plants the Jewels in my skin;
right in, in the vein, in the pulse in my soul
- I'm in a cascade
brighter than any local sun
-shine, snuck in the waterfall
of Faith Hope and Love

'm dizzy, crying tear buds of light
in the clear water looking at me,
covering covering covering:
over and over, I know that I
know, am fully known, and
so loved.

~

the hours, are seconds,
whats left to ask, know,
think, be -

Grace grins,
" You'll see
you'll see."

~

Grace and Faith, Hope and Love
such words, like Hind's feet
in High places

~

20. River Of Light

i pray and a river falls out of me

it runs un noticed by our
feet, and faces, our ports,
harbours and markets places
the Stream bathes deserts
Orion, Jupiters moon & Mars;
also our bars raising falling,
we prisoners of Hope, of
harvests cluttered with empty
wells & beggars for peace,
running away to war; by the
stream of clear river, nay this
Double River - with trees on
each side, I sit. My ears are
my prayers. Here He does a
thing I cannot forget. Here
in the river of Light, He washes
my feet, and pleads, " Do this

for each other, if You love Me."

" Why?"

"Because if you don't love one
another, Lies will win you. But
Dove-bel, love one another."

Wash everyone's feet? That's insane
I shrink thinking of all the people that did
what they did and I forgive them, but this
is too close for comfort. This is a
footstool at their mercy,

He silence is the bare roof of ones
gone too long. His Eyes sweep the
'forgotten' verandas of God. He takes the stench
off my reserves of waste, my ache for personal rain,
"Soldiers prepare for drought.." He says

Am 360 degrees blest to be this loved,
but am no soldier, Sir God, just going to
be a special needs' kids' teacher,
I like Warden Ma, but some others I better
forget!

"My Jewels, you've asked who they are?
They are these, the billion kadzillion
clusters of every man,
woman and child..."

Whaaaatt, even
those that treat others
like a TOCE TASU....those?

"Alright, 'Outcastes' , ha
specially
those...."

(Dorm sis?)
He nods, affirmative, loud as
many suns on waters in many earths,
(.. wants me go wash her feet now?)

"Yes, and even in your mind,
where you conceive or
give away your own
newborn, Love."

Did He just say what He said?
like I'm discarding
my
'newborn' love?

I want to object,
but His judgement
of others, is His
judgement of
me

bitter as the coarse garment on a Baby's
soft bruised
sacred
Head;

sigh,
if there is a colour
for Compassion,
that's the Bruise, He

leads the filthy rags, I still carry inside my
me'
by His waters, still rushing to me
He bathes too, the roots of everyone
in me -

neighbour, peoples, children,
earth

lonesomeness
isolation
habit
patterns

thought these were my tears
falling in my face but they're His,
2 millenniums old

I, sit by that
double tide and His
Daddy- eyes,
here there is one
Season of the Soul –
Restoration

~

May I be a shadow of Your Dew -
write me a letter in Light,
ink my thought, with Your
Mind

~

21. Polished Arrow

&
stem
is shaved
of twig, bark,
flower of self-d
-estruct, the Archer,
removes ===till the Shaft
is ready fr
Arrowhead
Nock, and
Fletcher=>
Hidden in
t' Quiver +
seasoned
by circum-
-stance ////
toughened
for ....targ
-et, ...the Po
-lished ....Ar
-row--------------------->

"EMA,"

His voice startles the cobwebs
that so quick try to rebuild
their castles in my head,
"Would it be too small a thing
to visit one person, a potential
Dove-Bel, and since we're
using Illustrations- you are now
my Polished Arrow, so please
complete one pending.........?"

It is a loaded command, He is not
backing down. I thought He was as
gentle as a Dove & only for me -

He is thinking of Dorm Sis.

It is 8 am, horror hour. Breakfast
DS is in organdie sari, all 7 yards
hemmed with hand - made lace, Oi. It is
her birthday, I shut my shivers
and wish her.

First she stares, then laughs, we hug a small
birthday hug, and wait for her acidic tongue to

go whichever way it normally whiches, but
today she smiles,

what do I say..... Dorm Sis is melting, she's an
iceberg, slip, sliding,
like me. Oh the fabulous melting of insults
in their Awkward. We shape-shift, she's
as startled as I -

melting our sleeves and fingers,
onto the long table with steel plates, tumblers for 20+
 coffees steaming small clouds over
idlis 'n coconut chutney, like an
uncalculated Emotion-
'Strength' is a word too much for human powers;
our icebergs slide out the
mosaic floor cluttered with
everyone and
Warden's tiny toes in
blue Hawaii slippers furious -
how dare the water pump,
overflow with so little spring underneath-
her curls shine in almond oil, and in her ears pulled by
white stone earring-rays,
they flash signals, beep beep
beep : even Warden is a
a mighty lighthouse, I haven't seen before? DS

and I, all of us, wash our
20x10 = 200 fingers by
stainless steel tap heads, they turn
anthems of fresh water springs, goin gon
under our feet -

everything can change, in a day,
in a moment.
'You don't have to feel something
 to understand it.' someone said. The scent of 9 am Light
here is our new gardener shaving the guava tree,
for pruning,

~

am taking that Post with the Special Babies
this is clear as the Light in my cathedral
of Dears;

a Dear Stranger
gave me Hind's feet in
the worst places, we have 4 potholes in the
gullies behind our House of Joy, we have Mynas
clacking beak in mango trees by the park, there's an
Eatery, a Parlour - here some days we wash our crowns
in herbal shampoo; I look in glass windows by a local
croton garden, its yard full of gold scarlet cashew leaf,

or turning orange rust before monsoon -

we are torn maybe,
but fantastically,

only the Light Untouchable-
we, so tiny in the Gaze of Eternity,
& loved, so loved. His Beauty for my
ashes. Impossible, yet in the cosmic
Quiver of God, my purpose is to
'Be-loved', and to Love.

..

..

You saw thru'
the shutters of my
mind: when I was a child was
scared of coat-hangers, now I am
grown, I see the universe in mustard
lil seeds, of Faith ~ growing tall tree-
yellow buds Rain falling in my sun-

flowers turn *turn, turning* to You. I,
we,Your Polished Arrow kept for
purpose, unforgotten,
never alone.

"From the body of my birth
He made me for purpose."
adapted, Isaiah 49, the Bible

midnight tells dawn,
'You're dead gone.'
Dawn says nothing,
just Rises.

~

www.ingramcontent.com/pod-product-compliance
Lightning Source LLC
Chambersburg PA
CBHW071340140726
47996CB00005B/2058